COLONIAL PEOPLE

The Colonial Dressmaker

LAURA L. SULLIVAN

Cavendish
Square
New York

Published in 2016 by Cavendish Square Publishing, LLC
243 5th Avenue, Suite 136, New York, NY 10016

Copyright © 2016 by Cavendish Square Publishing, LLC

First Edition

Website: cavendishsq.com

This publication represents the opinions and views of the author based on his or her personal experience, knowledge, and research. The information in this book serves as a general guide only. The author and publisher have used their best efforts in preparing this book and disclaim liability rising directly or indirectly from the use and application of this book.

CPSIA Compliance Information: Batch #WS15CSQ

All websites were available and accurate when this book was sent to press.

Library of Congress Cataloging-in-Publication Data

Sullivan, Laura L., 1974-
The colonial dressmaker / Laura L. Sullivan.
pages cm. — (Colonial people)
Includes bibliographical references and index.
ISBN 978-1-50260-482-8 (hardcover) ISBN 978-1-50260-483-5 (ebook)
1. Dressmaking—United States—History—18th century—Juvenile literature.
2. Dressmakers—United States—History—18th century—Juvenile literature. I. Title.

TT504.4.S85 2016
646.409'033—dc23

2015005585

Editorial Director: David McNamara
Editor: Andrew Coddington
Copy Editor: Cynthia Roby
Art Director: Jeff Talbot
Designer: Stephanie Flecha
Senior Production Manager: Jennifer Ryder-Talbot
Production Editor: Renni Johnson
Photo Research: J8 Media

The photographs in this book are used by permission and through the courtesy of: Public domain/Jozef Israëls - The young seamstress - Google Art Project.jpg/Wikimedia Commons, cover; The Colonial Williamsburg Foundation, 4; Public domain/After George Gower/File:Elizabeth I George Gower.jpg/Wikimedia Commons, 7; Public domain/File:Marijona Chmara.jpg/Wikimedia Commons, 8; Nordisk familjebok/File:Dräkt, Fransk adelsdam, Nordisk familjebok.png/Wikimedia Commons, 11; Alexsvirid/Shutterstock.com, 12; Public domain/Polly Bedford/File:1791 sampler.jpg/Wikipedia, the free encyclopedia, 14; The Colonial Williamsburg Foundation, 17; Public domain/File:François Boucher - The Milliner (The Morning) - WGA02892.jpg/Wikimedia Commons, 18; The Colonial Williamsburg Foundation, 21, 23; Travel Bug/Shutterstock.com, 25; The Colonial Williamsburg Foundation, 29; Anagoria/File:1730 Seidenkleid mit Spitzenmuster anagoria.jpg/Wikimedia Commons, 31; The Colonial Williamsburg Foundation, 32, 34; The Colonial Williamsburg Foundation, Gift of Mrs. R. Keith Kane & Daughters, 39; Public domain/File:1793-1778-contrast-wholeplate-lowQ.jpg/Wikipedia, the free encyclopedia, 41.

Printed in the United States of America

CONTENTS

ONE

Women's Fashion in Colonial America

When the earliest English settlers established Jamestown in the colony of Virginia in 1607, fashion was among the last things on their minds. They were **speculators**, hoping to find riches in the New World. They brought everything with them from England and were too busy focusing on survival to worry about clothing as anything more than protection from the elements. In the early years, many of the settlers died from starvation and disease.

The First Colonial Women

Dressmaking wasn't an issue for the first Jamestown **colonists**, because there weren't any women among the settlers. The first two English women arrived in the colonies in 1608 with the second

Dressmaking has been an important part of colonial life since the first female colonists arrived in 1608.

wave of supply ships and new settlers. Thomas Forrest, whose occupation was only listed as "gentleman," brought his wife Anne Forrest and her maid, the fourteen-year-old Anne Buras. Within a year the young maid got married, and thus—probably—began the dressmaking industry in colonial America.

Twenty more women arrived in August 1609, and another hundred came a few months later. After a while, women were an important part of colonial society. Though the culture was **patriarchal**—men dominated most professions, owned most property, and made most decisions—women gradually carved out their own niches. One of the few professions open to a woman was that of **dressmaker**.

English Fashion

Initially, most clothing came ready-made from England on the supply ships that arrived with greater frequency. Fashion was highly influenced by styles in England. During this period there were many changes in women's garments.

When the colonists first arrived, the **ruff** was a popular ornament. Both women and men would wear fabric or **lace** ruffles around their necks. With the discovery of **starch**, ruffs could get very large, sometimes standing out as much as a foot from all sides of the wearer's neck. Some even had to be supported on wire frames.

Women's dresses in the early 1600s tended to have a narrow line, tight sleeves, and a deeply pointed waist. These tight, restrictive clothes were not at all practical for the life of a hardworking colonial

woman. But then, very few women's fashions were designed with comfort and efficiency in mind. Upper-class women didn't have to perform much physical labor. Lower-class women often modified styles to accommodate the hard work they were expected to do.

As time went on, the style relaxed. Ruffs disappeared, replaced by soft **linen** or lace kerchiefs. Waistlines rose, and sleeves were worn in a full, draped style. Dress sleeves might be slashed to reveal a contrasting fabric underneath, or gathered at the elbow and lower arm to make a pouf of material.

When English colonists first came to the new world, the ruff, worn around the neck, was a popular—yet somewhat impractical—fashion accessory.

A Dress in Parts

In the first half of the seventeenth century, a dress consisted of separate parts. A **bodice** covered the torso like a tight jacket. It had tabs at the bottom, to which a skirt was attached with ties or pins. A roll of fabric, called a bum roll, was fastened around the hips to give the skirt volume. Often, the sleeves were separate, too.

The bodice might not quite meet across the front of the torso, allowing a woman to wear a decorative triangle called a **stomacher**. Fancy stomachers were covered with fine embroidery, lace, or pearls. They might be stitched into place over the **stays**, or actually laced to the bodice.

A woman wore two kinds of **petticoats**. One was an

For much of the colonial period, women wore stomachers, or decorative triangles that were attached to the front of their bodice.

undergarment; it was not meant to be seen. This was used to give the skirt shape and volume. The other petticoat was decorative, and meant to be seen. The skirt would be split down the front, allowing the petticoat—which was in a complimentary or contrasting fabric—to be viewed. Some skirts were closed in the front, in which case the woman would only wear the first type of petticoat as an undergarment.

The different parts of a dress were often interchangeable. This allowed a woman to change her look by switching out sleeves, skirt, petticoat, bodice, or stomacher. Women often asked their dressmakers to alter dresses to conform to new styles, rather than spending money on an entirely new outfit.

The Mantua

Just as today, fashions were always changing. Sometimes the waist was worn higher or lower. Sometimes the sleeves were tighter or fuller. Colonial women usually wore dresses that were a little behind the times. By the time a dress crossed the Atlantic, ladies in England were already wearing something different.

In the 1670s, women's fashions changed. Instead of the dress being made up of a separate bodice and skirt, dressmakers began to create **mantuas**. These one-piece gowns had originally been worn only indoors, as nightgowns or informal wear. Now the one-piece

Fashion Detective

Finding out what colonial women wore presents some special problems. For one thing, few articles of clothing survived to the present day. Portraits provide some clues, but they only show women wealthy enough to hire a painter. Also, there was a trend of being painted either in costumes as historical figures, or in elaborate indoor attire such as robes. So many portraits didn't show what women wore every day.

Women often passed on their clothes to friends or family after they died. Inventories made of a woman's possessions after her death would be valuable. The problem was that a married woman was not considered to be a separate person from her husband. When she died, she usually could not make a will, thus few lists of a woman's clothing possessions remain.

Women's clothing was sometimes listed in court records. In 1747, Hannah Proctor reported the theft of some of her clothes, including gowns of brocade (heavy fabric with a raised design), striped lustring (a glossy silk), green damask (silk or wool with a woven pattern), red taffeta, brown silk, calico (patterned cotton), linen, and gingham (striped cotton). The clothing of criminals and escaped slaves was also listed in newspapers and court records.

In colonial times, the petticoat was a decorative garment that was meant to be seen.

design was adapted for public life. The front of the mantua was usually open to display the decorative petticoat. Often the skirt was caught up to the hips or the rear of the body, revealing almost the entire petticoat.

Dresses for Rich and Poor

Well-to-do colonial women wanted to keep up with the fashions. Especially in big cities such as Philadelphia and Boston, women anxiously awaited news of the latest dress styles from England. They wanted to know what the ladies of the royal court were wearing, and make something similar. As the colonies prospered, there was an increased demand for dressmakers.

Of course, poor women needed clothing, too. Most women learned at least the basics of sewing, and could make simple, rough clothes for themselves and their families. In England and in the colonies, there was also a thriving secondhand clothing trade. As wealthy women discarded their outmoded dresses, they might give them to their servants, or to a used clothing dealer. Poorer women could buy rich women's hand-me-downs. Clothes might be passed on several times.

The poor often wore styles similar to the wealthy. Although cheaper, they were made from more durable materials.

TWO

Becoming a Dressmaker

The only widely accepted occupations for women during the colonial era were wife, mother, and homemaker. Though plenty of women found careers, whether out of necessity or ambition, most were raised with the idea that they were destined to work in the home taking care of their families. Their own mothers taught them the housewifely arts, such as cleaning, cooking, treating minor illnesses, and sewing.

A Universal Skill

Both upper- and lower-class women learned aspects of these arts. A wealthy woman would learn enough to supervise the servants, give them advice, plan menus, and perhaps manage the family budget. She would learn plain sewing, but probably wouldn't spend much time actually making garments or mending. She was more likely to learn decorative needlework, making beautifully embroidered objects.

Poorer women, though, learned to sew so they could make their families' clothes, as well as their own, from scratch. Almost all women gained at least a basic knowledge of sewing. Most started around the age of four, when their fingers were ready to learn precision. They would do simple basting stitches and eventually learn to make small, neat stitches. Left-handed girls were often forced to sew with their right hands— and thus rarely became good at sewing.

Fancy Stitches

Some girls made **samplers**, or pieces of embroidered cloth, showing off all of their stitches and techniques. These might have

Girls from both rich and poor families sometimes made elaborate samplers that showed off their creativity and skill in decorative embroidery.

alphabets, decorative stitches, and even pictures of people, animals, and scenes. Girls were very proud of their samplers.

These fancy stitches were of little use if a girl wanted to be a dressmaker. To make clothes, she had to sew simple stitches very well. She also had to know how to drape and fit fabric, and create flattering or functional designs.

The Dressmaker's Apprentice

There were several ways a woman could learn how to make dresses. Sometimes she learned from her mother. Or she might be essentially self-taught, learning tips from friends and other dressmakers. If she wanted more formal training, she might be apprenticed.

The old **apprentice** system in Europe was very formal, and only certain trades practiced it. Only a recognized master could take on an apprentice. But by the colonial era, and especially in colonial America, the apprentice system had become less formal. A young person wasn't necessarily bound to a certified master, but just to someone who was established in their trade.

A girl or young woman apprenticed to a dressmaker would generally sign a contract. She would be bound to learn from the dressmaker for a period of time, usually either up to seven years or until she turned twenty-one years old. During that time she would not be paid, though she often received room, board, and clothing from the dressmaker.

During her apprenticeship she would learn all the secrets of the dressmaking trade. She would learn the best stitches for a long-lasting dress. She would grow accustomed to making dresses without patterns by fitting the customer directly. The apprentice would learn which fabrics were best to use for specific purposes, and how to take advantage of the qualities of the materials to get the best effects.

More than Just Sewing

Particularly if she hoped to eventually set up shop for herself, the apprentice had to learn more than just dressmaking. She had to become skilled at customer service, learning how to read a customer's wishes, and how to guide her to clothing that was most suitable (or most expensive). She also had to learn the business side of the occupation. Skills such as basic arithmetic would allow her to calculate the costs of fabric and labor, and keep her accounts in good order. She might also learn about the import trade, and how to haggle with fabric merchants for the best deals.

After she finished her apprenticeship, she would be technically a **journeyman** (or journeywoman) and be able to work for pay. She might continue to work for her teacher, or set up shop for herself.

The Shift

The **shift** was the basic woman's undergarment. It was shaped like a large shirt or nightgown and pulled on over the head. The shift might be made of linen or cotton. Its main job was to protect the valuable dress from sweat stains and body odor. The shift could be easily washed and changed; the dress could not. A poor woman might own only one or two plain shifts, which she washed whenever she could. A wealthy woman would own many and change them often. Sometimes the cuffs or neckline of a shift were meant to be seen, and could be embroidered or decorated with lace. A shift was also called a smock or a chemise.

The shift was a woman's main undergarment in the colonial era.

Dressmaking could support a woman and help her support her family. But a woman who wanted true financial success would strive to set herself up as a **milliner**.

An apprentice dressmaker might hope to set herself up as a milliner—and make far more money.

THREE

The Dressmaker's Day

For most of the colonial period, dressmakers were referred to as "mantua makers," for the one-piece dress style that was popular at the time. But the real profit was not to be made from mantua making alone. The true expense wasn't the labor, but the cost of materials. A woman paying to have a dress made might bring her own fabric to the mantua maker. Or the dressmaker might pick out the fabric for the woman. For that, she visited the milliner. A dressmaker with a little capital and a knack for business might be able to set up her own milliner shop, and make far more money selling fabric and other goods in addition to making dresses.

The Colonial Businesswoman

A woman had few economic choices in colonial America. Women might own a shop if they were widows, inheriting the business from their late husbands. Records from the era show that almost the only store a woman could buy and establish for herself was a milliner shop. It could be extremely lucrative. In the colonial era, people spent a larger percentage of their income on clothing than they do today. Dresses were not only necessary, they were one of the main ways a woman could demonstrate her wealth and position in society.

A Variety of Wares

The milliner's shop was the department store of the day. A milliner would sell ribbons, lace, and ruffles. She also had ready-made items such as caps, neckerchiefs, and the linen shifts that all women wore beneath their clothes. There would be cloaks, hoods, and muffs for the cold weather. She sold hats, and often trimmed them herself. (In more recent times, the term milliner usually refers exclusively to a person who makes and sells hats.)

She even stocked a few items for men, such as shirts. Some milliners branched out to other imported items such as jewelry, watches, and silverware. It really was a multipurpose shop. Many milliners were mantua makers. If they were not, they employed one or several mantua makers to work for them.

The Latest Styles

When a customer entered the dressmaker's or milliner's shop, she was greeted warmly. Perhaps she had come only to have a dress made or altered. But very likely, once inside, she would be tempted with the multitude of other items for sale.

The fashionable colonial woman was always anxious for news of the latest English and French styles, and the dressmaker was happy

Milliners and dressmakers had dolls that displayed the latest London fashions.

to oblige. She might have printed pages with depictions of what London ladies were wearing. She even had fashion babies—little dolls dressed in miniature versions of the most current fashions from across the Atlantic. These were shipped to her directly from London. Since most of her fabrics and ready-made goods came from there, she had many contacts in that fashionable city.

When the customer came in to the shop, she would see many drawers and boxes, but only a few items were on display. The precious items and costly fabric were tucked away to protect them from dust and dirt and only taken out for a serious customer. The customer might be tempted by a new hat or cap, but eventually she would remember her primary reason for the visit: to order a new mantua.

Designing the Dress

First, the customer would discuss the dress she wanted with the dressmaker. She might have some ideas of her own but would probably be influenced by the dressmaker's expertise. The customer could bring her own fabric, perhaps some fine silk she'd had sent from London. But the dressmaker was happiest if she bought the fabric from her own shop. The cloth was very expensive, and the dressmaker or milliner made a nice profit off its sale.

Unlike **tailors**, the dressmaker didn't work from a pattern or even take measurements. Instead, the customer's body modeled the pattern. The clothes were fitted, draped, and pinned on her body so they would conform perfectly to her proportions.

Stays

A lady always wore her stays while being fitted for her dress. The stays, or corset, was not the tightly laced, uncomfortable article of clothing that became popular in the

The mantua maker created her dresses directly on the customer's body, without using patterns or measurements.

nineteenth century. While later corsets could actually bend ribs and damage organs, the colonial stays were a relatively comfortable support garment.

Stays covered the torso from the armpit to the waist, and were used not just to control the figure, but to support the body and ensure good posture. Some modern reenactors who wear colonial stays describe them as comfortable. Even very young children, male and female, were given soft, lightly laced stays when they were learning to walk. This encouraged them to stand up straight.

The stays were such an important part of getting the right fit that customers sometimes sent the garment to the dressmaker instead of staying for several fittings. If the dressmaker was skilled, she could make an entire mantua from the stays alone.

The Final Gown

Ideally, the customer would return for three fittings. A very experienced mantua maker (or one who had several assistants) advertised that she could make a complete gown in one day. It took about ten hours of labor for a skilled dressmaker to complete a plain mantua. A more complex ensemble could take much longer.

When the gown was ready, the customer would return for a final fitting, and then pay. A dressmaker might serve a very wealthy

When the gown was finished, the customer was ready to attend a fashionable party.

lady in her own home, saving her the trouble of traveling. Before the dressmaker was paid, she might try to tempt the customer with more of her many wares. She might suggest that a new lace fan from Paris would complement her new outfit. Or she might hold up ribbons and garters to convince the customer to add them on to her order.

Although some dressmakers printed notices in newspapers, a satisfied customer was the best advertisement. When a woman saw a friend in a lovely gown, she would ask for the name of her dressmaker. Some women refused to tell, wanting to keep a particularly talented dressmaker all to themselves. But word usually got out, and a skilled dressmaker got plenty of business.

Sumptuary Laws

The earliest colonists thought it was important to be able to tell a person's position in society by their clothes. They didn't think it was right that an uneducated or poor person could put on fancy clothing and pass for a lady or gentleman. So they passed sumptuary laws, regulations about who could wear expensive clothes.

At various times in the early colonial period, laws were passed prohibiting anyone possessing less than 200 British pounds sterling (307.29 US dollars) to wear expensive lace, silver or gold buttons, or silk. People were brought to court for violating these laws. One man was fined ten shillings after his daughter was seen proudly wearing a silk scarf.

After a few decades, though, lawmakers abandoned the laws. No one was obeying them, and they were hard to enforce. Visitors from Europe often commented that colonial women seemed to dress above their station in life, and that even servants and slaves were often dressed in fancy clothing.

Making Old Dresses Look New

Dressmakers didn't just create new gowns—they also altered old ones. Fashions changed very quickly, and it was much less expensive to redesign a dress rather than to get material for a new one. A gown could be dyed to change its color. Lace cuffs and ruffles could be added or removed. A dressmaker could whip up a new petticoat or stomacher faster than a new dress, and this was enough to change the look. Sometimes, the entire dress was taken apart and the material was sewn together again in a completely new style. Even wealthy women disguised old dresses as new.

Dresses for the Poor

Poor women had dresses too, of course. A poor woman was usually her own dressmaker, or else she bought her clothing ready-made. Often the basic cut would be similar to that of a rich woman's dress. The style might be out of date—a farmwoman might still be wearing a separate bodice and skirt when the town women wore a one-piece mantua. The fabric was different, too, being plainer and not as brightly dyed. Even poor women usually wore stays. A woman working on a farm on a hot day might try to keep cool by only wearing a sleeveless bodice or plain stays with her skirt or petticoat.

A poor woman would do many repairs to her dress to keep it functional for as long as possible. She would wear her clothes until they wore out, or she might leave them to her daughters or friends after her death.

FOUR

The Dressmaker's Community

Whether she was a milliner with her own shop, or simply a mantua maker, the dressmaker relied on overseas trade to keep her business flourishing. Almost all fabric was imported from England or elsewhere. Very little material was made in the American colonies. Even when the raw ingredients—such as cotton, flax (which was made into linen), or indigo (which was used for a blue dye)—came from the colonies, it was usually sent back to England for processing.

A dressmaker had to negotiate the import business world. If she bought her own material, she had to bargain with merchants who traveled by ship across the Atlantic. She might even make deals with cloth merchants in London, using messengers or letters. The shipping industry was absolutely vital to the dressmaker's trade. It not only

Fabric was the most expensive part of a dress. It was far more costly than the labor involved in creating it.

carried material for her to craft into new gowns, it also carried news of the latest fashions. This spurred business as fashionable women clamored to have the newest styles.

Wool

Each type of fabric the dressmaker used was part of a specific industry. Wool generally began on a sheep farm in England or Ireland. Depending on the variety, one sheep can yield between two and thirty pounds of wool every year. The shorn wool was cleaned of dirt, and a natural oily substance called lanolin. It would then be spun into threads or yarn using a hand spindle or a spinning wheel. Traditionally, women were spinners.

Next came the task of weaving wool into cloth using a loom. In earlier times, weaving was a man's job, and was often a one-man industry. The weaver would even travel from village to village, turning the women's spun wool into fabric. In the 1700s, though, the first mechanization began. Cloth was made in factories by many people, women and men, working together. By the time of the Industrial Revolution in England (circa 1760 to the mid-1800s) cloth became less expensive to make.

Cotton and Linen

People in the eighteenth century became more interested in being clean and wanted fabrics that were easily washable. Cotton was the perfect choice. The fabric could be dyed with bright colors and patterns, and it was much lighter and more comfortable in the hotter regions of the colonies than wool. Cotton was grown worldwide, but it was usually processed into fabrics such as chintz and calico in England and shipped to the colonies.

Linen, made from the flax plant, was often used for undergarments because it is so light and cool. It also gets softer the more it is washed. However, linen is labor-intensive to make and tended to be expensive. It could be blended with wool to make the popular colonial fabric linsey-woolsey.

Silk

By far the most luxurious fabric a dressmaker could work with was silk. Though colonial Americans tried to establish a domestic silk industry, it was not successful. Silk is made by the silkworm caterpillar. These insects feed exclusively on mulberry leaves. They weave their cocoons from silk fibers in a single long strand. When the cocoons are

The silk for this gown was woven from strands produced by thousands of silkworms.

boiled, the silk strand is loosened and can be unwound. Thousands of silkworms are killed to make a pound of silk. Silk used in the colonies was mostly produced in Italy, Spain, and France.

Tailors

There were other kinds of clothing manufacturers in the colonies that also provided accessories to complete the colonial woman's outfit. These manufacturers might have competed with dressmakers

A tailor created garments that were more fitted, such as riding habits and stays.

for business. A poorer woman might have to choose between a new dress and new shoes, while a wealthier woman would want it all. Therefore these clothing industries complemented each other.

Today, a tailor is generally a person who makes men's clothes. In colonial times, he was a clothing maker who relied on patterns and precise measurements to craft garments. He would make certain women's garments, such as the more structured riding habits, which usually resembled men's clothes, but with a skirt instead of breeches. The tailor also made stays.

Shoemakers

The profession of shoemaker was sometimes divided into cordwainer, and cobbler. The cordwainers made fine shoes from leather. Cobblers repaired shoes. Often, the shoemakers specialized in making either women's or men's shoes. Ladies' shoes might also be made of velvet, satin, or silk, and were often decorated with embroidery, bows, or fancy buckles. Bright colors were popular, and many women liked red shoes. The left and right shoes were the same.

Lacemakers

Lace is a fabric that incorporates holes or open spaces to produce a decorative pattern. It can be made in a variety of ways. All of the

Women's Hats

If the dressmaker was also a milliner, she might have learned the art of trimming hats. Colonial women wore many styles. Women almost always wore a cap (also called a mobcap) over their hair. This looked a little like a cotton or linen shower cap, and protected the hair from dirt and dust. Over that she might wear a straw hat with a wide brim to protect her face from the sun.

A more fashionable hat might be covered with silk and decorated with flowers, ribbons, or lace. Women with elaborate and high hairstyles would wear a calash. This hat looked like a hood, and was made of silk or other material mounted on a stiff frame so that it was almost like a helmet.

Young girls wore caps alone, or styles similar to their mothers. Young children wore pudding caps—padded hats that acted as helmets to protect their heads as they were learning to walk. It was thought they would get "pudding head," or permanent soft spots, if they hit their heads while young. Later, "pudding head" was slang for a foolish person.

Women almost always wore a cap or bonnet and sometimes wore a hat over it.

methods require precision and are very time consuming, so lace was a luxury item. Still, it was one of favorite trims in colonial times, for both men and women.

Most lace purchased in colonial America was made in Europe, either in England or in France. The most expensive kind was needle lace, made with a needle and thread. Bobbin lace, made by twisting and braiding threads together, was slightly less expensive. Lace could be made with cotton, silk, or linen threads. It could even be made out of fine threads of silver or gold. The dressmaker had to have contacts with lacemakers or lace merchants to be sure she always had a supply for her dresses.

Jewelers

Most jewelry was imported from Europe. Necklaces tended to be short and high on the neck. Pearls were a favorite, and many necklaces were worn in the choker style. Necklaces and bracelets weren't made with metal clasps but were fastened with ribbons and bows.

Though diamonds, rubies, and emeralds were highly valued, the biggest trade was in costume jewelry. False diamonds made of glass were called paste. A mix of zinc and copper that looked like gold was called pinchbeck.

FIVE

The Dressmaker's Legacy

The eighteenth century was the beginning of the true fashion industry, and the dressmaker was at the forefront. Prior to that time, only the elite could set trends, or afford to follow them. All but the simplest clothing was prohibitively expensive. Anyone could look at a person's clothes and know, at a glance, their exact social and economic status.

Fashion Equality

However, in the 1700s, clothing became less expensive. Expanding empires provided an abundance of raw materials. A gradual increase in industrialization and the use of factory methods rather than individual craftsmen brought down the prices of cloth, lace, and other components of fashion. For the first time it was possible for the middle classes to acquire less-expensive versions of what the rich were wearing. Eventually, most people couldn't tell whether a person was a duchess or a successful merchant's wife simply by her gown. Even the poor and working classes tended to dress in the same style as the wealthy. These outfits, however, were fewer and made of cheaper, usually sturdier fabric.

The increasing equality of dress was part of a trend toward equality across the board. It was part of the Age of Enlightenment, a period lasting through the 1780s that put the focus on the individual and his ability to be a rational, intelligent human, rather than relying on tradition, the church, or the aristocracy for guidance.

Revolutionary Changes

When the colonies declared their independence from Britain in the conflict known as the American Revolution, fashion—and many other aspects of life—underwent a radical change. In practical terms, trade with Britain was suddenly cut off. Dressmakers could no longer get the fabric, lace, and accessories that they had once imported from their mother country. Fashion gossip was no longer exchanged, so colonial women did not know what styles to imitate.

What's more, England was now the enemy, so colonial ladies didn't want to look as if they had just come from London. During the war, for the first time, nearly everything in America was strictly,

authentically American. The British blockade made sure that America couldn't even trade with the countries, such as France, that supported its fight for independence.

Clothing, for both men and women, became a way to demonstrate their patriotism, or love for their country. Abigail Adams (wife of John Adams, the first vice president, and second president of the United States) pointed out that the colonists "would wear canvas and undressed sheep skins, rather than submit to the unrighteous and ignominious

This gown, worn by First Lady Martha Washington's sister Elizabeth, is made of silk. It was first made in 1750. A few years before the Revolutionary War, in 1770, it was redesigned, probably because England's restrictive import policies made new silk cloth hard to come by.

domination" of the British. By making purely American styles, using local materials, and altering old gowns rather than making new ones, the colonial dressmaker was in her own way contributing to the fight for independence.

A More Simple Style

Just before the American Revolutionary War, women's dresses had grown to extravagant sizes. They had hoops to hold the skirts out in a ring, or panniers that sat on the hips and made the skirt extremely wide from side to side (though flat at the front and back.) Women added to this look with very high-heeled shoes, ruffles, big hats, and huge hairstyles. It was the dressmaker's job to make colonial women look as impressive and fancy as possible.

Following the war, though, the look changed dramatically. Hoops and panniers disappeared, and the dressmaker crafted dresses with narrower, sleeker lines. Hairstyles flattened, heels lowered, and fabrics became less gaudy.

Now that America had (at least for a while) broken ties with England, it turned to France for both imports and fashion inspiration. France had been through its own revolution from 1789 to 1799. With cries of *liberte*, *egalite*, and *fraternite*, (freedom, equality, and brotherhood) the French cast off their monarchy in a bloody revolution

After the American Revolutionary War, fashion changed dramatically, with people favoring simpler styles (left) over elaborate ones (right).

that led to the death of much of that country's aristocracy, including the king and queen, and thousands of civilians.

The French no longer wanted to dress like the despised nobles. Instead, women adopted a simple style of gown with a high waist and a narrow skirt. They were made of light, clinging materials.

The Original Fashion Victim

Some of the fashion trends after the two revolutions have macabre origins. Some people believe that the simple new dresses, resembling nightgowns, were modeled after the shifts people were forced to wear on their way to the guillotine. It became fashionable to wear a single red ribbon around the neck, symbolizing the line of blood from the executioner's blade. There was even a new hairstyle, *a la victime*, or in the style of the victim. A woman's hair was cut very short, exposing the neck as it would have been before an execution. It was then brushed forward to make it stand up in messy spikes. That fashion didn't last long in the United States, but some women definitely adopted it for a few years.

American fashion followed suit, and before long most of the women in the new states wore simple dresses made of lightweight material that hugged the body.

American Homespun

Fashions would continue to change through the generations. Big skirts and compressed waists made a comeback, but the idea of homespun American clothing continued. American fashion became known for its individualism. Though dressmakers used imported goods, they also used domestic fabrics, which tended to be a little coarser than European ones.

While dressmakers continued to make luxurious gowns, they also made dresses more suited to the American way of life. Americans were explorers and pioneers—they needed dresses that were fashionable yet durable, and cut for an active lifestyle. Though America has always been at the forefront of fashion, its specialty was, and is, popular and functional fashion. It was the colonial dressmakers who set this trend.

Glossary

apprentice	A person bound to learn a trade from a master for a fixed period of years, usually with little or no pay.
bodice	The vest-like part of a woman's dress that is above the waist.
calico	Cotton cloth which has been printed with a design on one side.
colonists	People who have settled in a colony, or distant area that is controlled by another country.
dressmaker	A person who designs and sews dresses, and sometimes other pieces of women's attire.
journeyman	The stage after apprenticeship but before becoming a master; a journeyman could be paid for his work.
lace	An open fabric, usually expensive, made by looping or twisting cotton or silk thread into patterns.
linen	A soft fabric made from the fibers of the flax plant.
mantua	A one-piece gown worn over a partially exposed petticoat.
milliner	In colonial times, a person who owned a store specializing in women's clothing and accessories; later, a hatmaker.
mobcap	Also called a cap, a soft hat with a decorative ruffle that covers all or part of the hair; a hat was often worn on top of the mobcap.
patriarchal	A system, society, or government that is controlled by males.
petticoat	A skirt that might be worn as either an undergarment or a visible decorative garment under a draped overskirt.
portrait	A drawing or painting depicting a person.
ruff	A starched frill of lace or other material worn around the neck in the sixteenth and seventeenth centuries.

sampler	An embroidered piece which shows off the sewer's talent. It often includes fancy stitches, alphabets, mottoes, etc.
shift	An undergarment made of cotton or linen which is shaped like a shirt or tunic.
silk	An expensive, fine fabric made from fibers produced by the silkworm.
speculator	A person who makes an investment or takes a risk, hoping it will pay off later.
starch	A spray or powder that is applied to clothes to stiffen them.
stays	A laced undergarment extending from under the arms to the waist or hip area, used to provide support for the body, or to shape the body; also called a corset.
stomacher	A decorative triangle of material attached to the front of a bodice.
tailor	A person who crafts clothing using patterns and careful measurements; often specifically a maker of men's suits.

Find Out More

BOOKS

Miller, Brandon Marie. *Dressed for the Occasion: What Americans Wore 1620-1970.* Minneapolis, MN: Lerner Publishing, 1999.

Raum, Elizabeth. *The Scoop on Clothes, Homes, and Daily Life in Colonial America.* Minneapolis, MN: Capstone Press, 2011.

Walker, Niki, and Bobbi Kalman. *The Milliner.* New York: Crabtree Publishing, 2002.

WEBSITES

Kid Info

www.kidinfo.com/american_history/colonization_colonial_life.html

This site's section on life in colonial America has many topics to choose from, including several articles on dressmaking and colonial fashion.

US History

www.ushistory.org/us/index.asp

Find out all about the history of the place now known as the United States, from pre-Columbian times to today.

MUSEUMS

The American Textile History Museum

www.athm.org

This affiliate of the Smithsonian documents and celebrates the history of textiles and fabric in America from its earliest days to today.

Colonial Williamsburg

www.history.org

This living history museum in Williamsburg, Virginia, recreates an entire colonial city. The 301-acre (121.8-hectare) site has many original historic buildings, and actor/docents who reenact colonial life, including dressmakers, milliners, tailors, shoemakers, and more. The website is also full of valuable information about the era.

Index

Page numbers in **boldface** are illustrations. Entries in **boldface** are glossary terms.

About the Author

Laura L. Sullivan is the author of many fiction and nonfiction books for children, including the fantasy *Under the Green Hill* and the romance *Love by the Morning Star*. She has also co-written the upcoming romantic mystery *Girl About Town*, set in the Golden Age of Hollywood, with famed director and producer Adam Shankman. She is the author of many books for Cavendish Square, including six titles in the Colonial People series.